D0271757

READING POWER

Record-Breaking Animals

The Giraffe
World's Tallest Animal

Joy Paige

The Rosen Publishing Group's
PowerKids Press™
New York

Published in 2002 by The Rosen Publishing Group, Inc.
29 East 21st Street, New York, NY 10010

First Edition

Book Design: Sam Jordan

Photo Credits: Cover © Artville; pp. 5, 7, 12–13, 15, 17, 19, 21 © Indexstock; pp. 9, 11 © Animals Animals

Paige, Joy.
The giraffe : world's tallest animal / by Joy Paige.
    p. cm. – (Record-Breaking Animals)
Includes bibliographical references and index.
ISBN 0-8239-5964-3 (lib. bdg.)
1. Giraffe–Juvenile literature. [1. Giraffe.] I. Title.
QL737.U56 P35 2002
599.638–dc21

                                    2001000169

Manufactured in the United States of America

Contents

Giraffes

Giraffes are tall animals. They live in Africa.

Africa

Giraffes are taller than some trees.

Giraffes are 6 feet tall at birth. They grow about an inch each day. Giraffes can grow to be 18 feet tall.

Eating

Giraffes have very long necks. Their long necks help them get food. Giraffes eat the leaves from the tall trees.

Giraffes also have long tongues. Their tongues are 18 inches long! Their tongues help them rip the leaves from the trees.

13

It is hard for giraffes to reach water. They must spread their legs to drink.

The Tallest Animal

Giraffes have long legs. Their long legs help them run fast. Giraffes can run up to 35 miles an hour.

Giraffes also have very good eyes. They can see for miles. They can smell and hear well, too.

Giraffes are taller than any other animal. They are more than 10 feet taller than zebras. They are the tallest of all animals.

Glossary

Africa (**af**-ruh-kuh) the second-largest continent in the world

birth (**berth**) when a baby is born

grow (**groh**) to get bigger

miles (**mylz**) units of measuring distance, equal to 5,280 feet each

reach (**reech**) to stretch out and get something

Resources

Books

Giraffes
by Emilie U. Lepthien
Children's Press (1997)

Giraffes
by John Bonnett Wexo
The Creative Company (1999)

Web Site

Animal Shenanigans Presents: The Giraffe
http://gustown.com/giraffe/rae12.html

Index

Word Count: 153

Note to Librarians, Teachers, and Parents

If reading is a challenge, Reading Power is a solution! Reading Power is perfect for readers who want high-interest subject matter at an accessible reading level. These fact-filled, photo-illustrated books are designed for readers who want straightforward vocabulary, engaging topics, and a manageable reading experience. With clear picture/text correspondence, leveled Reading Power books put the reader in charge. Now readers have the power to get the information they want and the skills they need in a user-friendly format.